Download New York State of Mind 1.0 FREE!

There are hundreds of interviews and dozens of **Behind The Music Tales** series books to follow.

That's why I am giving you a copy of New York State of Mind 1.0 for FREE!

Get exclusive 1992 and 1993 interviews with Tragedy Khadafi, Brand Nubian, and Pete Rock & C.L. Smooth FREE!

I am only looking for your email. You will receive emails with updates on new releases, exclusive images, original audio, and be eligible for free advance copies of series books. You can opt out at any time.

http://eepurl.com/cj-cvb

Behind The Music Tales Books

N.W.A: The Aftermath

The Real Eminem: Broke City Trash Rapper

The Real Destiny's Child: The Writing's On The

Wall New York State of Mind 1.0

Magnolia: Home of tha Soldiers (Behind the Scenes with the Cash Money Millionaires)   The Real 213

The Real MC Eiht: Geah!

The Real Diddy

The Real Daft Punk

Praise for Harris Rosen

This guy! I plead the fifth. This guy is nuts."
- Eminem

"Dope questions, man. Very insightful, very thoughtful."
- Guru (Gang Starr)

"You like a Psychiatrist or some shit? This shit is just coming out but go ahead."
- Mary J. Blige

"Definitely a real interview! Digging deep up in there, man. Not afraid to ask questions!"
- K-Ci Hailey (Jodeci)

"The Wizard asked me for a copy of your magazine."
- Guy-Manuel de Homem-Christo (Daft Punk)

"You didn't wear your glasses and you haven't carried your hearing aid. What else is wrong with you?"
- Bushwick Bill

"Peace and blessing, Brother Harris. Thank you for inspiring my words. Keep 'yo balance."
- Erykah Badu

"Can I see that pen?"
- Bobby Brown

"What else do you want to know? Talk to me."
- Aaliyah

Behind The Music Tales 8.0

The Reasonings of Buju Banton, Bounty Killer & Sizzla

Exclusive Interviews & Photos

Harris Rosen

Copyright

© 2016 by Peace! Carving and Harris Rosen.

All rights reserved under International and Pan American Copyright Conventions. The Author has provided this e-book for your personal use only. It may not be resold or transferred to others. You may not make this e-book publicly available in any way. No part of this e-book may be reproduced or transmitted in any form by any means, electronic, mechanical, scanned, recording, or distributed in any printed, or audio form without written permission.

Published by Peace! Carving

First edition

First published in November 2016

ISBN: 978-0-9953072-5-4 (Print)

ISBN: 978-0-9953072-0-9 (Digital)

Mr. Heller Press

Heller HQ

QB

Spadina-Fort York

Toronto, ON m5v 2b3

Canada

Dedication

This series is dedicated to my son Louis, late father, mother, sister, grandmother & the late Raymond Wallace.

Thank you for a lifetime of support and encouragement. I would not be here without you.

Acknowledgments

I wish to personally thank the following people for their contributions to my inspiration and knowledge and other help in creating this book:

Mark Reed, Rob Harris, Peter Cherniawski, Renae, Reid, Arty, Shahroze Ilyas, Ricky Rufus, Mark Saldeba, Ian Steaman, Eon Sinclair, Jr., Todd DeKoker, Phil Demetro, Peter Lazanik, Rishi Persaud.

Contents

Preface 1

Chapter 1: The Practices, Principles, Philosophy & Reasonings
Of Buju Banton..9

Album Discography..24

Chapter 2: The Practices, Principles, Philosophy & Reasonings of Bounty
Killer..29

Album Discography..47

Chapter 3: The Practices, Principles, Philosophy & Reasonings
of Sizzla 49

Album Discography..86

Who Is Harris Rosen? 94
Other Books By Harris Rosen 95

Preface

Jamaica, Jamaica.

I began listening to Reggae music in 1991. Growing up in Toronto, it is impossible not to be affected by its driving rhythms and patois, especially when one is a Hip-Hop fan and the vast majority of the community are of Caribbean descent.

Over the years, I have visited Jamaica multiple times and travelled coast to coast taking in its majestic sights and sounds. From Spanish Town to Burnt Savannah; Red Hills and Mona; uptown and downtown parties; Sting and Studio One 50th anniversary; inside the homes and studios of its leading lights and legends.

The music and its culture are genuinely international experience. I will never forget entering the Lagos Hilton Hotel club in Lagos, Nigeria, and witnessing Dancehall Queens in action and meeting local artists who had booked tickets to Jamaica to further their career.

The Jamaican Dancehall of today has a rich lineage. One that has gradually transformed from the live bands and sound systems of the 40s and 50s to the record producers and don promoters of the 60s and 70s, through the age of digital in the 80s, then onward to the 90s and beyond.

Arthur "Duke" Reid's Trojan Sound and Sir Clement "Coxsone" Dodd's Studio One are revered worldwide for fueling the sound and creating an industry. Though without its unsung heroes the Art Form would be stuck in the mud.

Hedley Jones, perhaps the most unheralded pioneer in the history of the music, built the core of the entire industry. Jones made the first solid wood electric guitar in 1940, a full year before Les Paul constructed his prototype and seven years before he patented it.

A professional musician and licensed electronic technician, He was commissioned by hardware store owner Tom Wong in 1947 to create Jamaica's first full audio spectrum amplified sound system. Wong, a.k.a. Tom The Great Sebastian, acknowledged as the first Jamaican sound with a Toaster, then dominated the party scene. On the heels of Wong's success, Jones was commissioned to create separate sound systems for Duke Reid and Sir Coxsone Dodd.

Jones went on to implement Jamaica's first traffic lights in 1952, and the first double necked solid body electric guitar in 1961.

By 1963, Jamaican artists had begun to carve out a unique sound of their own. Savvy Reid and Dodd saw the future and started their record labels moving into producing and manufacturing. Jones was commissioned by Sir Coxsone Dodd to build the equipment for the iconic Studio One. His sound system electronics are fueling the dances and the recordings that played at them, notably the global symbol of all Jamaican music, Bob Marley.

***

As Reggae developed, so did its talents. An incursion of sound systems superseded the Toaster for the deejay and sound clashes as the message took a turn from societal issues to sex and gun talk. Over time the location where dances took place became a musical form itself known as Dancehall.

In the mid-80s, digital riddims took over on the heels of Lloyd James a.k.a. King Jammy, Casio MT-40 production of Wayne Smith's "(Under Me) Sleng Teng". Jammy hearkening back to the days of Hedley Jones earned his stripes as an electronic technician.

The 90s espoused the age of slackness as the beloved red, green and gold of the Rastafari made way for gold chains and ribald Dancehall Queens. Righteous conscious artists such as Garnett Silk, Tony Rebel and Ragga man Capleton balanced it out.

The digital rhythms then spread to the lucrative U.S. market on the backs of Shabba Ranks, Buju Banton, Chaka Demus and Pliers, and others.

Unfortunately, the music became overwrought with a litany of contradictions as it seemingly embraced western culture on the one hand and opposed it on the other, primarily manifested by its anti-gay rhetoric and ideology.

As a direct result, the music was shunned by many just as it had seemingly begun to crossover into mainstream acceptance. The major labels that had embraced the music and culture dropped offending artists from their rosters relegating them to the minor leagues of distributed labels and speciality store import orders.

***

Born Mark Anthony Myrie in Kingston, Jamaica, July 15, 1973, Buju Banton is a certified natural talent. His career began in 1988, and by 1992 his socio-political and hyper-sexual lyrical assaults reigned supreme. In 1992, He broke Bob Marley's record for number one singles in a calendar year with rapid-fire releases leading the charge for a new generation of artist and the ensuing age of slackness. Tunes such as the anti-gay "Boom Bye Bye" clashed head-on with "Batty Rider" and "Deportees" illustrating and agitating the mentality and sentiment of the time.

The poor and downtrodden people ate it up with vigour, as the ever-percolating undercurrent and climate of Jamaica continued to simmer.

The **Mr. Mention** album earned the best-selling album in Jamaican history in 1993, leading to a deal with Mercury Record. Voice of Jamaica followed in August 1993, marking his international major label debut. Then his inner circle came crashing down

Buju Banton lost close friends and peers DJ Pan Head, Dirtsman and Mickey Simpson in separate 1993 incidents setting him on the path to righteous and conscious life. The tragic December 1994 loss of beacon of light Garnett Silk weighed heavy too. It became the catalyst that completed his spiritual transformation and the full embrace of the Rastafari way of life.

The seminal classic ***'Til Shiloh*** released on July 18, 1995, and the world grasped his conscious message. Buju Banton could do no wrong, and indeed his status became somewhat celestial. He then maintained stable and steady year in and year out, both on the domestic and international scenes.

The Buju Banton interview featured here occurred in December 2003 at his Axum compound, home of Gargamel Recording Studio in Kingston, Jamaica, after a spliff and a hot Guinness.

At the time, Elephant Man was good to go. Sean Paul had the light. And if the dispute onstage that year's Sting International festivities were any indication, Vybz Kartel and Ninjaman continued dancehall's coup d'etat tradition of new blood clashing with old guards.

Chilling in his studio compound, you got the sense that Buju Banton had been there, done that. Granted, the lyrics factory wasn't working overtime, he'd never sold platinum, and since taking the dancehall crown from Shabba Ranks and then renouncing even metaphorical forms of violence after the 1993 murders of his friends, he'd been out of the clashing circuit.

Buju Banton had the fitness regimen required to live long and prosper in the dancehall, gladiator business or not.

***

Born Rodney Price in Kingston, Jamaica, June 12, 1972, Bounty Killer is known far and wide as The Warlord. From 1993 through 2003 his booming, commanding delivery, boss attitude and streetwise outlaw music laid claim to the top spot in the worldwide dancehall. A string of big tunes was hitting nonstop, his name on the tip of everyone's tongue. He was responsible for putting on Scare Dem and Elephant Man, Busy Signal, Wayne Marshall, Mavado, Vybz Kartel and others.

Outspoken and controversial, Bounty Killer had his share of battles in the Dancehall with Merciless and Vybz Kartel. However, his seemingly omnipresent war with Beenie Man is the most well known spanning clash albums, onstage battles and bad-mind towards each other until 2014, when they recorded the song "Legendary" together.

His most infamous song is his guest shot on No Doubt's "Hey Baby," which earned him a Grammy Award for Best Pop Performance by a Duo or Group with Vocal at the 45th Annual Awards show on February 23, 2003.

The Bounty Killer interview featured here occurred during the summer of 2002, inside a New York, New York hotel room before the release of his ***Ghetto Dictionary*** volumes - ***The Mystery*** and ***The Art of War*** on VP Records.

Bounty Killer spoke on the state of Reggae music and what was holding it back from crossing over to the masses. The difficulties of working with No Doubt on "Hey Baby" and its controversial video; He lashed out at his arch rival, Beenie Man, and named his top Sound Systems, artists, events, and strains of ganja.

***

Kingdoms rise, and Kingdoms fall. Over the past two decades, Sizzla has about out-ruled them all. Of the more recent heir-apparent cited by royal watchers in Reggae music's global dancehall culture - a man like Garnett Silk, Capleton, Buju Banton, Bounty Killer and Beenie Man, none have ascended the throne as high as the one known by his loyal subjects in Jamaica and around the world as Kalonji.

Born Miguel Orlando Collins in Kingston Jamaica, April 17, 1976, and raised by devout Rasta parents in the August Town district of East Kingston, Sizzla first began spreading his homeschooling by way of the microphone as a teenage DJ for the Caveman Hi-Fi Soundsystem. But it wasn't until 1994 when his initial studio sessions with Fattis Burrell yielded hit after hit on the Xtreminator label, that Jamaicans first realised the scope of what was yet to come.

Sizzla has released over 60 albums and commands respect around the world for his musical offerings. He has embraced and engaged countless youth with his spiritual Rastafarian teachings and lifestyle educating them on corruption, oppression and how to uplift themselves and their people.

The Sizzla interview featured here occurred in Toronto, Canada, before his sold-out show in December 2005. The photos shot on Christmas Eve 2003 inside his Kingston, Jamaica, Judgement Yard compound. Sizzla and crew had no plans to commemorate the birth of Jesus Christ.

***

Buju Banton, Bounty Killer and Sizzla have all experienced backlash from the LGBT community for their anti-gay lyrical stance.

It will come as no surprise to their legion of fans and those who grew up listening to them dominate the international Dancehall, where they toiled at the top of the charts and on the tip of everyone's tongue for decades, that each is raw and candid with absolutely no filter.

It must be overstated that the opinions expressed here on homosexuals are not socially acceptable or politically correct in this world and many will not appreciate seeing them in print. They exist here as a historical document of the times and the prevailing sentiment in Jamaica where the conduct is outlawed to this day.

The international LGBT movement banded together as one voice and lashed back illustrating their unified might and force. They pressured Embassies and High Commissions, who are "morally obligated" to refuse working VISAS to artists who dare to violate and spread hate.

Despite the extent of their success and conscious state of mind, the legacy of "Boom Bye Bye" and bad spirit towards the LGBT community continued to haunt them and exact its revenge. Throughout their storied careers, each was pursued by an omnipresent cadre of LGBT rights activists everywhere He performed outside of Jamaica, and eventually, it significantly cut down on the number of live performances and cash flow.

In December 2009, Buju Banton was arrested in an undercover cocaine sting. Reportedly setup and recorded on tape stating that he could broker the deal. Detained for testing the merchandise in a Florida warehouse with 7 kilos on-site. Sentenced to ten years for conspiracy to possess and distribute cocaine. Many denials and appeals later he remains locked up in prison with a December 2018 release date. The world yearns for his voice.

Though Buju Banton, Bounty Killer and Sizzla have experienced the loss of significant opportunities and income by being denied travel VISAS, and the Jamaican government banned talk of the sentiment due to the international outcry, none have retracted their words.

Disclaimer

Opinions expressed in the interviews are not necessarily those of the Author. A few are not socially acceptable or politically correct in this world, and many will not appreciate seeing them in print. However, they exist here as a historical document of the times.

Chapter 1

The Practices, Principles, Philosophy & Reasonings Of Buju Banton

Jamaica is always referred to as a violent country with unrest permeating the air, due to its intricate hierarchy of a divided class system and the socio-political allegiances of respective Parish councils. Anything goes, and life can flip on a dime. It was alleged the Police killed 133 people in 2002. In June 2003, the longtime party in power, The People's National Party's run of four consecutive terms abruptly ended when the opposition Jamaica Labour Party captured 12 out of 13 Parish's in elections.

Kingston is a city that prides itself on a good party and the Holiday season performs like none other bringing together the best and most live events of the year. Billed as the Greatest One Night Reggae & Dancehall Show on Earth, **Sting International** or *Reggae Sting* occurs every December 26th inside Jamworld Portmore. Banding together all the top artists of the day, with a proper selection of gold performers and bonafide legends. It's infamous take no prisoners live clash is arguably the most anticipated stage show of the year. Promoter, Isaiah Laing, is the one time most feared Police Detective in Kingston. [In 2013 he published his autobiography '**Point Blank Range, A Jamaican Bad Man Police — the story of Isaiah Laing**'].

On December 26, 2003, the behaviour of *Reggae Sting* performers and its audience steadily crossed the line from orally abusive to violent. There were the usual gunshots in the air; A female audience member was struck by a bottle indiscriminately chucked by a performer; The lyrical clash between Ninjaman and Vybz Kartel erupted into a melee. One moment Ninja was pacing the stage like, well, a Ninja, in full graduation day dress. The next moment Vybz Kartel and three of his cronies decided to rush him and reach for the mic; Bounty Killer walked out before his performance over a contractual dispute upon discovering he would not close the show; The audience bottled the stage and pandemonium ensued.

It was not a right situation, and there was even talk by the Promoters themselves that the event may be cancelled for good. The day after the 2003 edition of Sting, we entered Buju Banton's Axum compound, the home of Gargamel Recording Studio. We found him relaxing with a few friends and received a warm welcome. One of our crew blessed him with a new pure-breed dog, and the offering truly touched him.

He gave us a personal tour of the studio, and then we sat outside as Buju Banton engaged us with his somewhat celestial revelations.

***

What is on Buju's mind these days? What are you working?

Buju Banton:
I just finished working on some singles. I'm still working in studio. This is my recording studio. First of all, let me welcome you to Axum, Gargamel Recording Studio. Let me welcome you. This is I and I establishment where we produce music. Right now I'm working on my next album which is slated to be released by March.

What's the album about? What message are you bringing across?

Buju Banton:
My message is one universal, and that will never change. I will not omit consciousness from my works.

As Buju Banton, you're always one of five artists associated with Reggae internationally, universally. Why are people believing in you? Why is your name carrying on?

Buju Banton:
I have made a sacrifice ever since I was a youth. Low the moon was just above my head, but I chose the love of God instead, and I gave my love instead. Instead of taking the moon. In other words. I could have touched the world. But, simplicity is a thing that you cannot get when you're on top. You have to be humble from the beginning and know that the foundation of what you're trying to the prostate is whatsit. It's one of humbleness, y'understand? So, therefore, the music that I and I sing people can identify with it here, across the world, universally. The love that I and I feel, the love that I and I is trying to express can also identify with that. I keep it real.

How has the music progressed over the years?

Buju Banton:
The progression of the music has been one which one can pinpoint and put their finger on. I am very happy with the progress.

I give thanks and praise to Almighty God who inspires all. For me to come from nowhere this day and be the person who I am with the knowledge of the world that I now possess, and I have the way to function. I give thanks for this everyday joy, for this music to open my eyes because it is indeed the greatest teacher. It is my teacher.

What do you have in mind? What do you want to get out there?

Buju Banton:
There's so much things to say right now, so much things to say. The world suffers. The masses of the people suffer. Knowledge is power. The Black man still finds himself not reading enough. Therefore, our work will not seize until the globe is educated and love is in the heart of mankind, and the world realises that this is all our backyard. The whole Earth. So there's no need to drop a bomb nowhere and create a crater unnecessarily and devastate lives.

Where does Buju fit into the whole scheme of things?

Buju Banton:
I see myself as a spoke in this wheel which has many spokes. But, I am the spoke who continue to turn, never bent, never break, never bow, and take a solemn vow to deliver the people no matter how long.

Jamaica is a very culturally rich and righteous island and as they say where there is good there is also evil in equal amounts to balance it off, correct?

Buju Banton:
Well, in every scenario there will be good, and there will be evil. There will be rich, and there will be poor. There will be justice and injustice. But one must find common ground in all of this, finally. A way where we can communicate and get rid of the negativity that is holding us back.

There are those who say music is from the Devil.

Buju Banton:
I don't want to talk about that because I don't want nothing to do with the Devil.

What do you think of what went on at ***Sting***?

Buju Banton:
What went on at Sting was most disgraceful to the Art Form, which I myself have worked so hard to prostrate over many years. It is also an embarrassment on a wide scale to us as entertainers and the patrons, and knowing that even though I wasn't a part of it nor was I a part of the billing.

I do apologise to the patrons on behalf of my coworkers because whatever one does the chain reaction goes on.

What should happen to those artists who are involved?

Buju Banton:
Well, disciplinary actions should be taken, and one should know that this is not a joke business nor is it a gladiator business. It's more of a business to unite the nation and bring them to a firm meditation in irieation. Man cannot beat man this day. Man does not have such power. But the most high God Almighty seeth all things and lo and behold this is his music.

Do you feel it was odd for an event that was run by a prominent Police Officer, for the artists that he hires to perform to be shooting onstage?

Buju Banton:
There wasn't any shooting on stage. Don't get it twisted.

What is the real story?

Buju Banton:
It was just a very Yankee like melee. You know when rappers get down and throw down similar scenario. No gunshots were fired on stage. So don't get it twisted when you go back and make your report. Likewise to all international media, don't get it twisted, beef happens. Right now the biggest beef is 50 Cent and this guy's name - Ja Rule. We don't want the same scenario here in Jamaica to escalate any time at all. So do not add fury nor fire to the fuel.

Do Producers appropriately treat Jamaican artists?

Buju Banton:
I cannot speak for the majority but I know I control my corner and whatever I do I control it to the max, and I control how I'm treated. So, therefore, I treat people with respect and hope that they will usher the same.

Who is distributing your upcoming March album?

Buju Banton:
Well, hopefully, VP will be the recipient of this one again.

Do you feel that your music is adequately promoted?

Buju Banton:
No, and you know that Buju Banton will always receive a little fire because of "Boom Bye Bye" and all those things associated with my past. Nonetheless, I do not look for open arms to rush and embrace my product. Nonetheless, I will continue to do what I'm doing because there are people out there who believe in what I'm doing.

Do you regret "Boom Bye Bye"?

Buju Banton:
There's no regret in my life nor in my career because music is a joy. It is designed to uplift, educate and eradicate negativity from the minds of the people yet bring you closer to yourself.

Have you been asked that question 100,000 times before?

Buju Banton:
Yeah, well, I don't fuck with it anymore because I'm not into that. The faggots already know where me stand already. I am the rebel who they will love to hate.

Would you speak to the effect of American music on Reggae and vice versa?

Buju Banton:
It's reciprocal. We both learn from each other, vice versa.

In the last few years, Buju Banton is on the rise again.

Buju Banton:
I've never gone anywhere. Throughout my entire career, I've managed to maintain my career. I don't believe in being on top. I believe in staying in the pack. I want to make room for the upcoming artists at all time. I see myself as someone who people must not become tired of. I myself hate monotony, so therefore I space my work. I always try to make good work, so people can appreciate it when it does reach them.

What is Buju's purpose?

Buju Banton:
My purpose is one which no word can define it; it's celestial, rather celestial.

Have you been to outer space?

Buju Banton:
Yeah, many a times.

What did you discover when you were there?

Buju Banton:
That the world is a beautiful place from above.

What planet were you?

Buju Banton:
Well, I was in Bujumania! Seen! And that planet is where love exists, no war survive. Democracy has a true meaning there, not demonocracy but democracy. Therefore, when I go on a planet, it is musical, and I try to invite other people to that small world of mine. Come on, let's enjoy it one more time.

When are you coming back to Canada?

Buju Banton:
Canada is a nice place, but the immigration and all these people give I a warm time whenever time I journey across these borders, and therefore I think it is strategically designed to keep I out. So, therefore, I don't venture too tough.

If you get a big cheque will you go?

Buju Banton:
Well, it's not a matter of cheque because I've been offered cheques. It's a matter of immigration knowing that Buju Banton is not here to pollute, nor to disrupt, nor to resolute, nor to smuggle, nor to juggle. But to play music for all people.

Do you come across that problem more in Canada than other countries?

Buju Banton:
Yeah, certainly.

Do you think it is racism, prejudice?

Buju Banton:
Well, it's a lot of things. Yeah, is a lot of things. Most of it is related to my past, but nevertheless, Canada is a place that I love and ... Mississauga, Dixie 401West; whole Massive Jane and Finch; Scarborough; Calgary crew; Montreal, Quebec; Ottawa; Winnipeg; Nova Scotia. Yeah, these places. Toronto, you're the great. I love these places, nice people.

What are your memories of Canada and Toronto?

Buju Banton:
I have some fond memories, great memories. One of my fondest memories was playing at the Skyline Hotel in Mississauga. It was a great event. But those were the great days.

Has the music changed over the past few years?

Buju Banton:
It has evolved, certainly.

Have the Promoters evolved -- has the business -

Buju Banton:
I don't know. I haven't been working in the circuit quite regular. The last time I've been there, I've been up in Vancouver three years in a row. When I travel through Seattle I go across to Vancouver and play the Commodore Ballroom three times, and the reception is great, the crowd turned out, sold out shows.

Are you putting out any new artists?

Buju Banton:
Right now we have the Gargamel label going strong. We just released some new tunes on the rhythm call the "Exciting Rhythm".
[Shouts out] Yo! What the new riddim we just released?
With Buju Banton and Ghost, Nuff Gyal, New Kids, Singer J; a whole lot of artists, this one is exciting; Bounty Killer.

What is the name of your sound?

Buju Banton:
My Sound is called Matrix Reloaded.

Why?

Buju Banton:
Numbers run the Earth, let's keep it there. Signs and wonders.

Like the Kabbalah?

Buju Banton:
Numbers run the earth, signs and wonders.

Do you want to school the people?

Buju Banton:
You possess the knowledge. He who is ignorant make yourself knowledgeable. The rhythm is called the "Notorious Jig."

STUDIO ONE 50TH ANNIVERSARY SHOW, NOVEMBER 27, 2004, 'OL COAL WHARF, PORT ROYAL, JAMAICA

Who do you like out there right now?

Buju Banton:
Everybody, as long they're saying something that is worthwhile. And this is our new label which we are coming out with Abijah's.

Do you have a clean version?

Buju Banton:
Of what?

So you can put it on the radio.

Buju Banton:
All my songs are clean. We don't make songs that cannot go on the radio. What else do you want to say to everybody? What else do you want to put out there?

Buju Banton:
I want to say to the people of Toronto, Canada, the people of the world who may put their blessing on this magazine and turn to the blessed teacher of which my article is featured. It's been a pleasure having you reading I, and I interview. I feel justified to know that people travel from far and wide to come and hear what I have to say in this small part of the Earth. Nevertheless, I do give thanks again unto the most high God almighty who make it all possible, and for you the people, each and every one of you. Whether you know me, whether you don't know me. Whether you love me, whether you do not. Whether you have heard me before, whether you have not. For those who haven't heard me before I hope that you will. For those who have heard me before: love. Continue to praise Jah. Continue to be good to your fellow man. Love begins with you first. You can't love anyone unless you love yourself, it is impossible, highly. Until we meet in the flesh. Goodness and mercy guide and protect. I, Mark Myrie, seh love always.

Harris Rosen

Behind the music inside the Axum compound and Gargarmel Studio.

Album Discography

1992

- **Stamina Daddy** (Techniques)
- **Mr. Mention** (Penthouse Records)

1993

- **Voice of Jamaica** (Mercury Records)

1995

- **'Til Shiloh** (Loose Cannon/Island/PolyGram)

1997

- **Inna Heights** (Germain/VP Records)

2000

- **Unchained Spirit** (ANTI/Epitaph Records)

2003

- **Friends for Life** (Atlantic/VP Records)

2006

- **Too Bad** (Gargamel Music)

2009

- **Rasta Got Soul** (Gargamel Music)

2010

- **Before the Dawn** (Gargamel Music)

2015

- **Special Edition** – EP

COMPILATIONS

2000

- **Dubbing With Banton** (Penthouse Records)

2001

- **Ultimate Collection** (Hip-O/Island Records)
- **The Early Years** (90-95) (Heartbeat)

2002

- **The Best Of** (Hip-O/Island Def Jam)

2004

- **Buju & Friends** (Penthouse/VP Records)

2006

- **The Best of Buju Banton** (Universal Canada)

2012

- **The Early Years "The Reality of Life"** (Penthouse/VP Records)

VIDEO

2002

- **Island Life (Live!!)** (CineVu/Downtown Entertainment)

Chapter 2

The Practices, Principles, Philosophy & Reasonings of Bounty Killer

The Poor People's Governor, Bounty Killer, rose out of the ghettos of Trenchtown, Riverton and Seaview Gardens. Beginning his life in the Dancehall as a youth under the eyes of his father, who operated and owned Black Scorpio Sound System. His transformation from boy to Bounty Hunter a badge of honour, the product of a stray bullet in the midst of a Parish political war on the walk home from school. From DJ to deejay, he touched many Sounds before connecting with Jammys, where he recorded for many years for both King and his brother, Uncle "T". His **Down In The Ghetto** album is a certified classic.

Branching off on his own, He launched the Scare Dem and Priceless labels. Embraced by the Hip-Hop community, He dove in and added healthy doses of beats and collaborations with Busta Rhymes, The Fugees, Raekwon and Jeru the Damaja on **My Xperience** in 1996, and Mobb Deep, Noreaga, Killah Priest, Cocoa Brovaz on **Next Millennium** in 1998.

2002 was, without a doubt, the height of Bounty Killer's career when He shared the stage with No Doubt at the Super Bowl half-time show for his guest shot on their multi-platinum hit, "Hey Baby". The song went on to earn a Grammy Award for Best Pop Performance by a Duo or Group with Vocal at the 45th Annual Awards show on February 23, 2003. However, it did not come without controversy and incidents, and Bounty Killer goes into detail on his behind the music tales here.

***

Which of your beef are true and which are fraud?

Bounty Killer:
Well, I had no true beef. All my beef is musical beef. Mostly in Jamaica the cats there, they never really have personal differences. It's musically because the people liked it, so cats deliberately go out to do that. It's not like they have a beef. It's just to get the hype. It's not a beef.

Are you friends with Moses? (Beenie Man)

Bounty Killer:
I'm not a friend with Moses, but me and Moses had nothing personally. We always use to hang together. We talked, whatever. I wouldn't say we're bredrens that I would tell my business or whatever, but we are all right.

We're business associates. We're musicians. We go to the same school but not in the same class. But, same school.

Elephant Man won entertainer of the year for the last two years. He's tight with you and a member of Scare Dem, who you put on. What if he comes to the number one position?

Bounty Killer:
No problem. The number one position is for everybody. Everybody has to be number one. The number one position was not made for one person. So, whatever the people wish or whatever the Almighty permits we have to work with it. It's not my ply or my cry to say I'm number one or to be number one. It's just nature. So, I bring Elephant, and he's a talented kid. I hope him the best, and I know he has it, so if he's to be number one, he's bound for that.

How have you been able to hold on to number one for so long?

Bounty Killer:
I don't even know because tell you what. I don't intentionally strive to hold number one. I just become number one. I guess what I do is so rated or it's so appreciated people say it's number one but I never intentionally try to be number one. I try to be the best of my ability and artistically, and it happens to be number one. So, I think it's me being true to my skills and myself because what I do from early stages of my career I continue to do. I keep my fan base from the early stage. I'm not one who keeps lost in time. I'm one who builds most times. My fan base kept growing. So, I guess that's what has kept me as number one because the root is there with the branch.

You're known as Poor People Governor, what are you currently doing in your community? How are you giving back?

Bounty Killer:
Well, I don't only give back to my community. I give back to the country where I'm from - Jamaica. I'm not one who feels like I'm from this community, so that's where I have to give something. I feel like the nearest person in need that's a blessing. So, I always try to do charity events. I always try to donate money. I always try to do free concerts. Whatever way I can do to generate funds to aid people. I also contribute some of the money to schools. I have a scholarship fund to put some kids through school, and a guy got shot at one of the events and died, and I put his little son on the charity event, and I gave him like $100,000, and I put him on the scholarship fund. We trying what we can do.

Are you signed to VP?

Bounty Killer:
No, it's just a one album thing. I'm not currently signed with anyone.

Over the last few albums, you've been building a Hip-Hop business.
I heard there's a new Bounty album in the works that you're trying to do, like big money, like a million dollars. Half Bounty, half to record the album. Do you want to say anything about that information briefly?

Bounty Killer:
No, I have no album in the pipeline. This is the album I had in the pipeline for like two years. I guess people expect that because they know we have the capability of that but that's not in the process right now. It's a possibility and I hope it happens because I need that budget to make a real album to show people the versatility and the skills of the artist. But that's not in the process now and we're not too excited about getting signed. As long as you have the raw talent record companies are going to see the talent and they are going to move to it. So now, I'm just focusing on getting myself visual. More exposure. More songs like "Hey Baby," and I got this new one just debut on 106 and Park yesterday. "Guilty" with Swizz Beatz. Yes, so these are the things I'm trying to do; get myself visual and then I will have the negotiating power. We have one coming up with Diana King too. It's called "Summer Breezin."

Is she back?

Bounty Killer:
Yeah, she's back. The album is called Back. (It was released as Respect on July 30, 2002) Her first single is "Summer Breezin'," and the video was just shot in Miami and it's done.

For the past six months, ever since the No Doubt video for "Hey Baby" came out. You've been dealing with gay community business, and everybody's saying this, that and the other. What have you learned?

Bounty Killer:
Well, that never really didn't teach me anything because all that happened I expected. They told me about that scene after I shoot my part and I told them this wasn't relevant. We sing about hey baby girls and all those things. We don't need a guy to be taking off his clothes. That shit was something literally Adrian [No Doubt drummer Adrian Young] did all the time. The video was definitely about being on the road, touring, girls being backstage trying to get with the guys and all them stuff. So they were just trying to recreate what they do on the streets and on the road when they are touring, and that's what Adrian does. So it was nothing with the intention of breaking anybody's stride, and then Beenie Man took it the other way. Beenie Man needed a point against Bounty because Bounty has been sledging him from '93. So I understand when he does that and he's desperate. At this moment he has no current hit song in the Dancehall nor overseas, nowhere. He hasn't been active for like two years. So he needs a break, so he just tries to use that, but as you see three months after where it is at now? No one speaks about it because it's not a reality. It was a real fiction. That was just a myth to me. I never appreciate it, but it's nothing to defy Bounty Killer. It was a scene different from the scene I'm in. I understand it was in the same video, but it was a different scene, and like you have one whole movie, several different scenes in the movie, and you can't use one scene to overlap a next scene. You have some people who appear in a movie, and he never comes back. So he's not the star of the movie and the movie isn't built around him. He hasn't even walked by, stood by in the movie. You can't say they are the star, and when the movie ends, we don't remember them. So Bounty and Gwen were the stars of the movie. I wonder why Beenie kept remembering this naked guy?

At the beginning when "Hey Baby" first came out. I was visiting Jamaica, and you were on TV doing great significant interviews, and I saw you on Sting. Then after a while, you stopped dealing with them, and you didn't do the Billboard Awards, and you didn't do critical events with them, and then all of a sudden you performed at the Super Bowl? What happened to get Bounty back on deck with No Doubt?

Bounty Killer:
They called Bounty. They called me, and I said, 'Okay, well …' I expressed my anger. They realised how upset I am. The fact was not to boycott the song and not do no promotions. The plan was to let them know how much I'm upset because the video came out, and I told them you have to get that out of the video before Beenie done any song or anything, and they let the video keep playing until Beenie done his song. And then they called me to do the NBC live, and I said, 'No, I'm upset.' People were saying you might go on stage and that cat takes off his clothes and that was irritating now because I was going to be live and this guy would take off his clothes I would smack him. That would be absurd for Bounty. So I said no, it seems dangerous at this moment, and then they called back. So I realised, well, this is important, and it's not for just No Doubt. It's important for Bounty too. I guess we just got to let little people go ahead and speak their mind and we go ahead and do what we have to do. So I go ahead and do the Top of the Pops and the Super Bowl.

What is holding back Reggae music from crossing over to the mainstream? Do you feel it has anything to do -

Bounty Killer:
Marketing, promotion and the big budget. We're ain't getting that. If you notice with Beenie. He's signed to Virgin and if you look at Beenie Man's video, they're not looking like the real videos. They still look like some cheap Jamaican video.

Little x did that video with Mya, that was a good video.

Bounty Killer:
Yeah, but you can still see that this video is some Jamaican trying to get into the mainstream. I want to see a video look like a video fit in all formats.

I don't want you can look at it and say, 'Okay, they're trying, but I can tell it's some Jamaican cat.' I need a real budget. I need a Dave Meyers Bounty Killer video. I need a Hype Williams Bounty Killer video. A real Bounty Killer video not featuring no artists. Bounty Killer. And they market it and promote it just like a No Doubt. I know Reggae music has that power to break the band wherever it goes. If No Doubt could come and do a straight Reggae track. Because the beat is what defines what genre of music it is. If it is an R&B beat, it's an R&B song. If it's a Hip-Hop beat, it's a Hip-Hop beat song. So it's a Reggae beat it's a Reggae Dancehall song. Gwen did it, and it's a smash worldwide, easily. Nobody even questioned what music is this. So why when we do it it's not going to be a smash? Because it is not promoted and marketed in the region. I deliberately know that's what it is. That's a politics. When some other foreign group use Reggae we get, it accepted all over. When we use our Reggae, it's not accepted likewise, and that's total bullshit.

What about the language barrier?

Bounty Killer:
The language barrier is not the problem. Tell you what. Tthe people know about patois, and they know it's something they would have to get on to. They know it's an alternative, it's like a broken English. People sing Spanish and break in America so what about patois? Patois is closer to English. Patois is like breaking English. So I'm saying patois is not so hard to learn, and if they get that mainstream play every day, they will learn it. But if they only hear the song once every six months, you're not going to learn anything about it. I've seen people sing "Vida Loca" in Jamaica and they don't know what it means. But tell you what. That song is played so much until it just gets inclined.

I've witnessed Elephant Man live a few times, and his stage show at Reloaded made Ludacris look like an idiot. Why is he not on a major label? Why is Elephant on Greensleeves? I don't want to speak another man's business, but to me, I think he has all the crossover appeals and songs and...

Bounty Killer:
He got everything -- He needs a label. He needs a budget.

And it's there but why doesn't anybody grab - Are they scared? What's holding people back?

Bounty Killer:
I don't know. It seems like they turned up, I guess that's why. They must have been turned up. They use to do it. Back in the days, we got a few major shots.

Shabba Ranks and Super Cat was on Sony.

Bounty Killer:
Tiger. We got Ini Kimoze. We got Tony Rebel. We got a few artists with deals back in the day, and then everything just fell off.

What happened? Was it the gay community business?

Bounty Killer:
No! I don't think it was no chichi business 'caa... Tell you what. Tony Rebel never sung no chichi business. Tiger never sung any chichi business. Super Cat never sung any. I guess Buju did. Shabba did. So that would have affected them. But it wouldn't have affected the whole business, the whole industry.

But it did.

Bounty Killer:
Yeah, but what I'm saying is I don't think it's that particular issue. I think something affects the whole business but not just that particular chichi business because tell you what, there is a whole lot of Americans who don't like chichi. So even if chichi is so big in America, there are some people who are against chichi so much. So even that audience we would have had. And chichis can't tell us that we should condone their behaviours and their ways. I ain't going out of the way to describe a chichi or I ain't going to go out of my way to hurt a chichi, but if a chichi comes across my path, that's a dead chichi. They know that we Jamaicans we don't like chichi men. I'm not going to tell you to go out there and hate chichi or go and kill chichi, but you know we Jamaicans we don't like chichi. So chichi knows I don't like him. Don't come across my path. If you come across my path, you violate. I ain't going over to your path. Chichi man on his own doing his chichi business I'm cool. You come into Warlord yard with chichi business you just died, and that's only fair.

Who do you rate these days?

Bounty Killer:
There are a lot of cats that I rate from back in the days, and there are a few that I rate currently. I would say currently I rate cats like Cobra, Spragga; Elephant is my soldier so I have to rate him. I rate cats like Sizzla; Anthony B, but I don't like the type of lyrics he has started to speak today because it doesn't make any sense to what he has delivered previously.

Before he came off cultural in the song. All the old tunes are great. Now he's trying to come differently.

Bounty Killer:
Yeah, there's a lot of them. Yeah, weird - Young artist like Bling Dawg, Wayne Marshall. We're bringing them up, and there's a few more cats.

Who is overrated?

Bounty Killer:
Beenie Man is the biggest overrated artist. Beenie is not better than Elephant. What Beenie does Elephant does it better.

Picking on people's style and biting people's style, Beenie can't do that like Elephant. I think Beenie is a great performer, but he's not such a good artist. Artistically he had less, but entertainment wise he knows how to get a crowd hype and know how to get a crowd jumping. But how to make a great song that would be a classic piece of work of art, no. He doesn't have that. Check Beenie's catalogue. He had no classic songs. All his songs are like tolls. You pay as you go, play as you go, or, like smoke. You smoke, and the trash fell, and that's it. You got to get a next one. Beenie's song is like a high.

There's no substance.

Bounty Killer:
No substance in it and everybody knows. Even that Mya song, he had nothing in it. You don't want to hear that song five months after it came out. Now if you play back that Bounty Killer Fugees you're feeling that shit because it's hard. Now you play back that Mobb Deep Bounty Killer, it's not going to be the most current popular song, but you can feel the days and the era when it came out. It's going to bring back a whole vibes to you. That's what a song should do, mark the date. Songs are like dates. When a song comes out from the 70s, and you hear it back, you can remember exactly how it used to be in the 70's. This was the song that used to play and this is what we use to do.

You remixed "Fed Up".

Bounty Killer:
I'd never do that. They do that, and they like it.

But the lyrics are still the -

Bounty Killer:
The same thing.

The same thing that you listen to as they make sense…

Bounty Killer:
Okay, that's another significance now. They remixed "Fed Up" and put it on **Ghetto Dictionary**, and that's from 1996, **My Xperience**, and it still sounds like what I'm saying now. So that is the thing that I use against them. I can still capitalise on my old issue and make them modernise and feel like a

great song today. They have to keep finding other issues to say every day, so they have no fan base that's following a certain issue. The people who like to hear about social issues and people's problems and their situation. They kept following Bounty from '93, and they are not going to stop because Bounty kept discussing these things and then even other too. But I kept the main topic right there, and that's good. When you can have a song from '96, and you can put it amongst your 2002 catalogue, and it still sounds fresh and sounds like it makes sense that's good. You've been doing a good job.

Kardinal?

Bounty Killer:
Yeah, Kardinal?

Yes.

Bounty Killer:
Well, Kardinal is a great artist. I heard Kardinal on that first song "Bakardi Slang", and I said but this song, this should have some Jamaicans in it because what he's trying to get across is that we're trying to break. The patois equivalent to the Yankee slang, and he's breaking down everything. Telling you what the Yankee said and what it means in Jamaican and what Jamaican say and what it means in a Yankee world. So when I heard that song I was saying, 'Yow, this song is hot.' I like this song, and this is what we're trying to do. Break the ice. So, I was telling DJ Khaled, and he said, 'Okay. Yow, that's my man.' I said, 'Call him up. Let him know I want to do the remix.' When I suggested it he was excited about it too, and I said okay let it happen and we just do it. It was as simple as that. I just heard the song, and I know that this song needs some Jamaican cat and it would be so great that he got Bounty Killer on this song to bring across all the Jamaican slang, and it came out and people in Jamaica loved it. I think the biggest place in the world that song is Jamaica. The leading success for it is in Jamaica. He came to Delano's Revenge, and he ripped it with that song. We just did a next one for his new album. I think that one is going to be even bigger because that one is more commercial like. The first one was underground.

What Sounds do you rate these days?

Bounty Killer:
Like Sound Systems?

Yes.

Bounty Killer:
There ain't much too great Sounds today. I guess the older Sounds are better because they have more knowledge and they have more music. Sounds like Stone Love is the only Champion Sound. But you got Sounds like Renaissance; you got Tony Matterhorn, you got Fire Links, you have Hot Freq from New York. They always hold it down. You have a couple of them, but there are not too many great Sounds around. You have Bass Odyssey. They're some clash Sounds. You have Mighty Crown; you have Black Katt, you got Kilamanjaro. Commercially I would say Matterhorn, Renaissance, Stone Love. They are the top Sounds from Jamaica. They are the names heard all over the world, every time on the flyer.

What Sounds are overrated?

Bounty Killer:
They ain't getting much Sound rating now much less overrated. But, I couldn't say Stone Love is overrated because from the time they bring in Dancehall, from the 70s, 1972. You got to give them props for that. They are responsible. They are the heart of the Dancehall. Just for the time, they spent we got to give it. Even if they ain't playing the best records, but they spent the best time.

When you get paid for a Bounty dub does everybody get the same effort, or is it more of a love for your cousin?

Bounty Killer:
I guess my cousin, or my friend, it doesn't make a difference. It's just like a spiritual vibe. Who gives me the most vibes. Who tells me something to get me hyped. It's not the money because you can give me a million dollars and your dub is wack. It's like the vibe that I get. For instance, when I'm doing a Stone Love dub, it's just like from when I was a kid I used to reminisce doing a song for Stone Love as a kid. So, when I get the opportunity to do a Stone Love dub now, this is my dream.

PEACE SPECIAL SUMMER ISSUE

pepa

no162
FREE

Bounty Killer

It's like I'm living my dream. It's more than just doing a dub for another song. Tony Matterhorn is some Selector that is obsessed about Bounty Killer. He's a fanatic; he's all about Bounty Killer. So when I'm doing a Tony Matterhorn dub that's like doing my dub. It's like that. It's just the spiritual bond that we have. It's not like financially. The money can't do this because if I'm not in a good mood and I don't want to do a dub, you can't give me a million dollars to do that. So, I guess it's just some people that I got a good chemistry with. Their dubs always come out the better.

What are the essential events like Sting or Caribana in Toronto, or the World Clash? What events do you rate as crucial?

Bounty Killer:
I think Sting and Sumfest. Carifest is one. I think the German Fest is one too because that is another side of the world. We need festivals like those to break the ice for new artists. But like in local, I think Sting and Sumfest. They are the two most essential ones. In New York, Carifest is very essential. We have no other outdoor big Reggae Dancehall festival like that. I think the one in Germany does the same because Dancehall is just breaking in Germany now. It's great to have a Dancehall festival. There ain't much though. Reggae ain't getting much love all over the world at this moment. That's why we are here fighting so hard to break that ice.

So Bounty is just putting in his support?

Bounty Killer:
Yeah, I'm just putting in my support and I'm trying to take the culture and the lifestyle of the people with the music. That makes it more visual and it makes it more interesting. Too many time people come to America, break, and then they start to dilute the music. They start to make the type of music Americans would like. We make music that Jamaicans like and Americans find family oriented and they like it too. So its Americans getting to like what Jamaicans like. We're not making Jamaican music for Americans to like and then Jamaicans say, 'Shit, I don't like that.' That's why Jamaicans call you a sell out some of the times because they say, 'Shit, you reach to America and you start doing shit to suit Americans.

You don't remember where you're from.' I'd rather do for Jamaican people and then I do one for the crossover market, like that "Hey Baby" stuff. Yeah, I do that. That wasn't really a hard song for the Jamaican market but it do work in Jamaica too. Why didn't they look at it like a sell out though? Bounty Killer kept doing 50 other hits for Jamaica. So if he does one that sounds popcorn for America we're okay because we realise Bounty Killer is supporting. But when you have all your heart in that crossover effort, it looks sell out.

Where is the best high grade in the world?

Bounty Killer:
Well, the best high grade in the world is Jamaica. I've never smoked no weed stronger than Jamaican weed. I've seen nice weed all over the world, but it's Jamaica. You have good weed in Holland, good weed in L.A., good weed in New York, good weed in Miami. But tell you what. Jamaica is the leading place. The best thing you can ever get is something they call the Indica or something called Alaska. No skunk, no chronic, no hydro. You can't mess with that. Alaska and the Indica from Orange Hill, Kingston, Jamaica.

What else do you want to say, Killer? What else do you want to put out there?

Bounty Killer:
I want to let them know that the **Ghetto Dictionary** is finally here. Volume one and two. **Volume one The Mystery**, **Volume Two The Art of War**. It's a good album, and it's like a collector's item. It have a lot of previous hit, current hit and future hits and it's like an 'A' to 'Z' for the street. Ghetto life is not familiar to the world. It's familiar to the sufferers and the strugglers all over the world but we need the commercial audience to realise what's going on in the ghetto and they could understand. And if they can make a change, try and make a change. So this album is dedicated to the streets, the hopeless and the voiceless and the downpressed. Its old People's Governor, Bounty Killer. Street language. I think they should check it out it. It contains over 40+ tracks, like 46 tracks and it's good. One side is like the hard side of the ghetto. "Warlord", The Art of War. And the other side is like the mystery, the unsolved mystery and problems that we have. You know the ghetto. We never know what's going to happen tomorrow and it's hopeless.

So, it's in stores now, pick it up, check it out and I think they will get to like it. We got this joint with Swizz Beatz called "Guilty". The first single from his **G.H.E.T.T.O. Stories** album. He's coming out with some compilation album, some various artists. The first single dropped and the video premiered here yesterday on 106 and Park; good reviews. I guess we're going to have a good summer.

Album Discography

1993

- **Roots, Reality & Culture** (VP Records)
- **Jamaica's Most Wanted** (Greensleeves)

1994

- Bounty Killer & Beenie Man - **Face to Face** (VP Records)
- Bounty Killer Versus Beenie Man - **Guns Out** (Greensleeves)
- **Down In The Ghetto** (Greensleeves)

1995

- **No Argument** (Greensleeves)

1996

- **My Xperience** (TVT)

1997

- **Ghetto Gramma** (Greensleeves)

1998

- **Next Millennium** (Black Tools)
- **5th Element** (Blunt Recordings/TVT)

1999

- **Poor People's Governor** (92-96) (Jahmin' Records)

2002

- **Ghetto Dictionary: The Mystery** (VP Records)
- **Ghetto Dictionary: The Art of War** (VP Records)

2006

- **Nah No Mercy - The Warlord Scrolls** (VP Records)

2009

- **Raise Hell on Hellboy** (PayDay)

2015

- **Special Edition** (FM Records)

2016

- **Dancehall Hardcore** - (KS Digital)

Chapter 3
The Practices, Principles, Philosophy & Reasonings of Sizzla

If, as many of the "official" accounts would have you believe, that 1994 was the year Reggae got culture again, then Sizzla was doing much of the giving. Between then and now the Bobo Dread has released well over 200 singles and, perhaps, as many as 60 albums, each one of them a new leaf sprung from the Rasta roots first sewn in Reggae music over fifty years ago.

Even in Jamaica, where ten youths from each Parish are running their own lyrics factory from home, that's no small feat. But many of Sizzla's good deeds have mainly gone, if not totally, unnoticed by a global market that went deaf to any natural mystic in the air after Bob Marley's passing marked the end of their Reggae golden age. They say the message has changed. Sizzla proclaims that the word is still the same.

***

Sizzla:

Jah!

What have you been working on lately?

Sizzla:

I've been working on the DDMG [Damon Dash Music Group] album. Brand new coming out the studio, lead vocals Sizzla Kalonji.

What is the album about? Where are you taking it?

Sizzla:

I'm taking it four winds of the earth; east, west, north, south. Straight to the hearts of the people. Words of righteousness and solitude where you can relax and do your thing. Music is all about life. Music is about getting people together, Singers and players of instruments. If people could unite like the instruments, then create the music how lovely that would be.

What's on your mind when you're creating?

Sizzla:

Well, naturally creating music is just heights of cleanliness. You got to be meditating and clean things where you'd like to go, how you'd like people to be living, and to speak out on such rights. You claim such a card. Whatsoever you perceive for your mind your whole body will take unto it.

You're into the 40 album range. What now?

Sizzla:

I don't even know. I just put out a whole heap of music. I make new music. I lose track of that because anywhere me go if a youth love it and a station have a riddim, I hate when I hear a riddim, and I don't deh pon it. I got to be on that riddim! That's what we need. That's what I'm all about. I'm born in this music for eternity. Our ancestors are musicians.

Everybody in life has a purpose. Everybody in life has a meaning.

Sizzla:

Exactly. You must know that it's good over evil, so you stick to the good because the good lead you on the path of righteousness. The bad lead you on the path of destruction, and there's still man doing good and man doing bad.

Were you chosen?

Sizzla:
Based upon the knowledge of the people. The people decide whatsoever they want to say, and whatsoever they want to do, you know? Speaking for myself, I must be chosen to be speaking the words of God unto the people.
Yes, of course, we are chosen because it's life, and praise the living God I'm living.

You've put out many messages over the years. I'll leave it at that.

Sizzla:
No, no, no, man. Finish it, man.

Some of it is positive. Some of it is construed by others as negative, but you say you're always about positivity.

Sizzla:

Okay. It's all good. Words get its meaning according to how it is being used. If you have something good to say, say it, and if you're going to bash against something that's bad, you got to say it. You got to speak the word. Man born ruler. Man is literally ruler. The woman she follows and takes the orders of the man. So they tell you we are King. We're from Church and State, from Africa. That's our prophecies, that's our life, our philosophies, our culture, our tradition. Principles from Solomon lines go straight up. Me a man! Me have fi rule over my house. I have a Church, Kolada. My family is the last of the Kolada. The world I see, I say that's how the world is gonna be around I. So I always try to maintain it on a clean level, and you still got to be in judgment where your own family know they mustn't really cross over the bounds, because crossing over my bounds is not just only my bounds you are crossing. You're crossing over a family's bounds with principles, and you might not know, so you've got to maintain humility.

How do you keep your mind and head clear when you seemingly weight the world on your shoulders? I've been to Judgement Yard. You have a whole community of people who rely on you every day to put food in their mouths, shelter over their heads, clothes on their backs. How do you deal with that?

Sizzla:

Life is the greatest, you know? No matter the great circumstances of being true, when I return to home they just look pon me and say, 'See, King, you still have life.' That's the greatest. Some of the highest tradition of the ancestral people. Yes, life is the greatest. You got to do what you got to do. Do it positive and shine the light. Shining the light don't mean just because there's no camera bredren mi just shine the light like that. It's the way you do things. It's what you say. Shining a light what you stand for. Doesn't mean you might stand for real strict principles and you might execute it and destroy others. It's like education. You use it for the best knowledge and use it for the betterment of the people. I got to stay free because the people keep me free. I myself keep me free. Life keeps going on, even though we have certain things out there that really might at times burden you. It depends on what will burden you. The loss of my sheep burdens me. I need to see each and every one every day. That is why when I go to the earth I have so much joy because anywhere I go it's the same thing. If you come into Canada the immigration search you. Going up to New York them search me. Same thing going to Jamaica. Where me born they search me. Leaving Jamaica them still a search me. Who wouldn't have learned by now? So you must know. You got to stay the principles in the Earth; it exists, so the family must know it. If I don't stand and hold the principle amongst I self, so I can show them what keeps me free, they gonna show someplace out there and it's out there. Even if you have your youth, your son or your daughter, and they don't steer free and keep a free mind and learn to let certain things go, they gonna go out there, and the Police gonna be at your door.

Do you fear reprisals? They tried to kill Bob Marley. They killed Peter Tosh.

Sizzla:
We don't fear dem tings, man. Can't stop death, you know what I mean? Reprisal is nothing. You know me. That's futile for I. I praise a true and living God. Reprisal is just amongst dudes that don't want to stand up for truths and rights, man and want to pack up on the most high. You just got to praise and know that's it.

Has the political climate of Jamaica changed over the span of your life?

Sizzla:
Based upon the question you asked now about the political climate with Jamaica now, that will never change because that's coming from Westminster Laws who have been slaving I, and I tell you before anywhere they search I. So Westminster Law same way. It's always there. It's never gonna leave until we go home. That's how serious it is because other people might express themselves based upon them present day lifestyle, but me, I express myself based upon the past where I'm coming from because I can't forget my forefathers' laws and not only my forefathers' laws, God's laws before my forefathers. So you always have to flash to the past and flash forward and say, 'Yeah!' Calculate it down the line. I love the nation. I love my nation. I love everyone, that's why I can keep myself clean.

Have you ever had an extraterrestrial experience?

Sizzla:

Naturally, you know. Me just a natural youth who live natural upon the Earth. Just smoke the marijuana, praise life, and a natural inspiration come to I.

Where does this album you're working on fit into the body of your work?

Sizzla:

Well, this album is naturally the root, foundation of Sizzla, same way. The body of my work is always to keep the people in unity, keep them focused, and then natural help me to educate themselves. Be free with yourself because you can't be just ignorant of the fact, you got to go search for the truth. Analyze your substance. Know what you're doing. We know this is what the people need. This is the overstanding. Rastaman always tend to change the bad words to good words. What you must learn now is words get its meaning according to how it's being used. We live in Zion, live on the Earth, and meditate on Mount Zion, the heavenly situation around us. Earth is Heaven, Heaven is Earth. Man is God, woman is Goddess. When they all come together in love and unity chanting one God, one being, one destiny here in the world. Word is God. In the beginning was the word and the word dwell amongst man. We have to utilize the word to keep the people in love, to keep the people happy. So we now, as youth on the Earth, being educated towards whichever level we might reach. We try to be the best we can be putting across the music. That means that if I have the knowledge to do better, we could really, really, not even me, my parents then could afford to send me to school. Anywhere I reach that's where I reach. So this album is being called Overstanding, reaching out to the people. Make it so that elder people could love it and young people. It's a meditative album. It's I Ashanti Day, you know what I mean? If you're not sitting down and putting yourself on a higherance sometimes you won't even know about certain things in your house because you're moving too fast. So you have to still keep a conscious.

Just now we have a deal going with Dame Dash now, who is originally from the U.S. That's mainly their custom. We're from the Caribbean - you'll find you got a lot of that beats. Sometimes their beats are clean beats. Music is life. Music brings the people together. So when I go somewhere, and I see a few musicians I don't discard them. I keep quiet and say, 'Yeah, some man would use you to make money could sing with you and make money ourself.' Use the knowledge. Over the years, travelling around the earth being experienced by being amongst the people, you learn people life. You learn it every day. So when you put it out to the people in the music now, you know what they want and what they would like to hear on that level. To keep them on that, right. You can't be foolish when you travel the earth. People say, 'Yeah, Sizzla! We love this song, and we love that.' So you get a nice little blessing now. Something that the people likes, so it's crowning.

Does your label understand you, your mannerism, what you believe in, and your history?

Sizzla:
They wouldn't just understand me like that. They have to be living with me based upon their raising, based upon their studies, based upon my profession. The label is like a business, based upon my profession of business. They might understand it to that level, but they might not understand it to the root, where it's coming from. The people will, I and I must keep it focused.

What is Sizzla the man, who are you really, the essence of Sizzla?

Sizzla:

A natural man, like a Doctor. Same thing you go to school and you read and naturally the Doctor say, 'Okay, this man build up. This man is a living man.' Build the same. Cut me and see blood same way. That's Sizzla. Someone just want to see you live upright, be clean. Express yourself, don't be afraid, but be not disrespectful sod. Just be clean, be nice because we've got to live and stay on the realms where the words can be in tune with us. You can't live outside the realms of the words. You haffi be there to hear the words. The words go forth. Whoever say the words right will lead us. Ever since we've been blessed with this life our parents been sending us to school and even we ourselves decided to further educate ourselves. Where we go to get this education? How could we get it? How could it be transmitted over to us? The words have to be said in different context and style.

In the beginning was the words, but yet still we're the ones that study and know that is that who said the words right here, but still, we destroy the words or create the words. True dem say, 'Man must think good, live good, live clean with a free mind.' Whatsoever you speak the words that come from your tongue, beautiful. People, like I said before, say Sizzla sing about God, and we sing about girls and ting. That's nice, but you've got to overstand the level like I say before with the label. Music is not only something we might have that is spiritual. We use music for business also 'cause it's the honest way. That's the only way the world know Sizzla must be money, man. I take care of the youth. Sizzla sings and plays the wheel of music. That's one of the most honest things you could find on the world right now to feed people, the music, and the next thing, again, people follow the music. People ain't going to see the crowd of pagan.

Sizzla go pon the stage he supposed to rip it up. You going over there and there are gangsters who don't feel they are going to get away. Come on, look at me, how could I be? Mama loves dada, so why are you hiding from it? Mama loves dada. Why did the security search me? People can kill people, so we have to show that even though the security might be a million miles away, people over here will want to kill us as well. So do not play. Stay over there. It doesn't mean you should use weapons of cruelty to kill people. We are not into that. First law is love.

Love is the first law that can be read in the Bible. Everyday people say love. Love created I and I. Love is the first law. If you love something then you won't destroy it.

Is there a place a man can go and find books to read, to live a proper righteous life according to the laws?

Sizzla:
The library.

What books?

Sizzla:
What books? You have many books. Books I know, books I don't know – many books. I haven't finished reading all the books in the world. I have so many books to go back to Africa and read. I haven't even started as yet.

Have you been to Africa?

Sizzla:
Yeah, man. I've been to Ethiopia. When I got to the land of Ethiopia I was sorry it wasn't like the plane where I could fly the roof and jump out in a parachute. That would be nice going down, chill, easy.
War, mistrust, hate, deception destroys the entire world. People don't trust people anymore. So this is the main trust, I have to know you as a son. You have to know me, and I know you. You know Sizzla and say, 'Yeah man, that's Sizzla how yuh mean? I don't have to see or hear him; I want to know that's Sizzla.' Whether I'm there in the flesh yes or no, you're going to do good unto my people and say what? 'That's my good friend, man. Send him through because you rule the house. Anything that belongs to you that I see, as long as you and I are friends.' Why are you and I friends? Not just looking at each other. You have to know the ways and the characters, calculate yourself amongst each other and know what you are dealing with from what I'm dealing with. I don't have to be dealing with the same thing, but that doesn't mean we are going to war.
Yes, my friend, that's the way I trod. The trod and everything is nice, but at the same time if I don't speak for you to know who I am you won't know. I'm not dumb; I'm Solomon's son same way. So when I go through Earth people know that.

So if I don't sing they are going to say, 'Watch out for Sizzla. Don't you know he's with the son of David? What is he doing?' David is a warrior in the Bible. So sometimes when some Rastaman sees me, they say, 'You Sizzla, you're a gangster. You remind me of King David.' Rastaman knows what's going on, but people in the world might not know because they are not checking it that way because we've been around a long time, and as soon as the King goes missing enemies raid and loot and rape and steal.

I'm saying you need to shape up your family and hold a proper statical order on your family's life, so they can know what you hold over there is clean and just for over here also. That means no looting and raping will happen. Men know this, so if men aren't thinking right men give orders. Men have powers but don't know what orders to give. The day we find the medicine he says he has the medicine and more diseases. He now has more instruments which are able to make things, and it's gotten worse because his heart and mind are not clean. If I have a nation now that thinks like me, the King, and I think of cleanliness and love, how beautiful will the world be? Some are saying look at my next Emperor over there and say what's up Mr. Japan? I need something down here to farm on my land. It's not coming in a container like a small mediocre thing being sent in abundance. The day Solomon used to send a lot of gifts, and it was never an Angel, a Mosque, a Burberry cologne. We didn't have those things, frankincense and myrrh and some other colognes. We had different things. We are the same ones. Our forefathers, your forefathers' son, so we have to live and utilise the knowledge because it cannot be hidden. It's in the book.

Everything I and I do as Solomon's son everyone use it. Right now with how things in the world are going, the world is running wid war! Let me tell you one thing, the conquering lion prevails. There are places where certain things and when I go there with my Rasta flag, and they see it, they say wait, 'Isn't that Solomon's son? Where is he going? He always has money and is always singing, come, man. I got it from he was over there.'

What are you afraid of? He has given me, and I'm going for the rest, not to mention what I have at home. Because I started chopping down an entire mountain and it was gold. So what is better than to build the palace in the gold, or to chip down the palace? The little mountains are pulling up blocks around here. It is just a little thing I used to dig down anything in the Earth and build our Churches in the Earth and carve it out.

Carve out image; an image can't talk. Those in here the daddy, and put a statue there, the statue doesn't know anything. I don't deal with the dead I deal with the living. Everything that comes to me is done by living people. Even if they are wicked, they do it, and they don't know that they are doing something good. So I should say, 'Yow, look here and do good and don't know, ease off the bad.' Easy as that, done.

Do you want me to show you how easy it is? And God said let there be [pause], and there was [pause]. It didn't take one month. Come on; it's the same thing, let it go, okay. If you're not ready for that speed, you're not ready as yet. You still have to have a speed within things as well because even if you're coming through the airport and they search you, you still have to move at a speed or else the people behind you will say what is taking him so long, although they don't like the search. But, if you take too long to get searched they quarrel. I'm saying, but you don't want to search, you shouldn't go in the bag. He said, 'Come out the way, man,' and you say, 'Okay, but why are you digging up my things?' And they say yes to it.

You have to love them and laugh with them and say yow like a little movie, that's why the baby's so happy, and every day we beat the kids and say get out of the dirt, bash. Watch the television, go sit and watch the television and read the book. They read the book, and they watch the television. When you watch the television, you see Power Ranger and Star Trek. They 'psh psh psh' and they get the vibes, and if you put him there to watch it on the TV and he comes out PUFF, thump down somebody and you BUP, 'Go and watch the television! Go and read the book!' So how much better are we?

Everyone is love, man. We come from love. No matter how we been, he have love somewhere in his heart, somewhere on him there is love. It is love that has made us. Mama and dada made love. Everything comes through love, and these things are love. Everything is through love because we say, yeah man! And they gonna love it, and we could produce good songs; people buy it, one room of love. Everything is created by love. Everything is love. How does love come about? Real love, Alpha and Omega, the beginning, and the woman is without end. Once you have the woman, the source of life is always there. Any day we go behind that we are cursed, so we live by what God says and keep the Sabbath nigh, and here is how the Sabbath coincide with it now. If you have your girl and a next man messes around with her, he gets jealous. So that's how I see the Sabbath, although adultery and those things still fall into a place that still coincides with the man and the woman.

So God set out his thing a long, long time before the heathen. We don't have a problem, we live! And if you attack God we attack you; it's simple. We know who is God, God is our King. Once He sits on the throne, He is our King, and God has a government, and He has the Church, He has the defence. Is you must come and with your principles. Look at the roses. You love her; you give her roses. Roses has thorns on it that can stick her, and if you stick her with a pin during the course, you're not saying certain little Valentine's things. She quarrels, 'Aye, it stick mi!' But if you give her roses, she'll pinch around it and hold it. So wisdom, Jah is showing you that even though they are roses they can stick you, and you gave it to her? Why we choose it? What are you doing? Jah is showing you that you should know good, do good. In doing good, slipping, there's a little thorn to stick you.

I say it's as easy as God said, let there be light, and there was light. No hitch, no hesitation. You're wrong; you're wrong, you're right, you're right. Let it go, that's it, easy as that. Once you know it too, you manifest it by yourself and people can know it.

Guys are saying it's a computer thing happening. You and I are the biggest computers. Robot computer aren't working. Human computers are the best. We make them and even though you go on the computer right there if you don't type in words you don't get a code. Words, the same words which are in the alphabet, ABCD, you go to school and learn it, they put it on the computer. Look at the big thing on the computer, everybody in the world, you go and do your ABCs, and you find it easy. So it is love that rules it. If you don't have any love, it's not going to be calculated.

Babylon uses love to rule us. Even if Babylon is the beast and the wicked he uses love, which is our power. He steals from us and uses it on us. That's how it is. Whoever has an ear let him hear. Whoever has eyes let him see.

Read the Bible because it is one of the most important books. The Bible is the music.

You must find the Bible in the house, and you must find the music in the house. You must find the food; you must find the clothes. If you don't find anything else you must find the food, clothes, you must find the Bible, must find the music, and you must find a knife.

He's going to say he's protecting himself, but he'll still peel an orange with the knife. Then why now, how much power is a gun over a knife? Since I was born in my mother's house and using a knife, as this knife cuts me and I understood that if a knife cuts me I could cut off somebody's head with a knife and I still did not do that, and when I see a gun I rush after the gun, why? Stupid! As I talk about forks, forks can still kill, kill is still kill, but our minds rule us, and we are not ruling it in a sense that we know we are rulers, so it messes us up.

Our principles are there. Some men are wicked, and some wicked people are still around him, so he sets up some principle to catch the wicked. You see yourself as the little sheep who might not know that. So even though he is a wolf, you have the ruler for the wolf and know the wolf is wicked, so he sets principles for the wolf. So you will get trapped in the wolf trap too, and he governs you as a wolf because he is governing you from the principle. He won't look at you and say you're a sheep. He'll say, 'You are no sheep. You're a wolf; you're tricking me.'

100 years, how will he know you are not a wolf? The nation has to call out for HELP! What are you doing? I didn't know Daniel. What's up, Moses? What's up, Joseph? I didn't know it was Joseph. Pharaoh does not read his Bible. Pharaoh is just a ruler for the people who own the Bible, but Pharaoh is not reading his Bible. If Pharaoh read the Bible, he would know what's happening. Pharaoh simply came and got some things that Pharaoh's family use to read the Bible, but Pharaoh came and got the honeycomb now, so he's rolls with that. But the people who wrote the Bible know where it's coming from because they know my father's father. Your father's father's father knows my father's father's father. So if you're acting like a wolf and I'm acting like a fool we're both idiots. We see that was their time of ruling stupid. Rule right now. Right now we should continue to rule your kingdom and make sure it's beautiful. So when you wake up with your family you can say, 'Yow, King!' and just look up and say, 'Yow, what do you want?' In the same way, you relate to your neighbour you should relate to the nation. That's it; it's finished.

Moses come, Moses has to walk the bush. Everyone has to walk like Moses. So when the mass of the nation wakes up, it doesn't frighten me. Every man is a man of his own and a woman of her own and a child of her own or his own. But once you don't have the knowledge to recognise that we will know when he has the knowledge, we will still keep him, carry him. But once he has the knowledge, he knows what's happening. He has to move.

Black people nice. White people nice. Everybody people nice, they should live by the word of God. It's the God of Israel because the true and living God set it that way for them. They're not following. If I don't follow, who'll follow my father? If he's my father and I'm not following him how will he follow my father? They're following your dad. Why should I follow you man? I'm not following your dad either. Let's go! End up doing something bad. You have to follow my father if you and I are friends. When you see me following my father, you'll follow your father, but if I'm not following my father and you're not following your father, well, that straight, straight from the elder, that's how it goes.

So we do we reason? Outside on the Earth people don't want to increase their knowledge. If you should go to school, even though you might be a couple of decades ahead of your child, he has to learn 1 2 3, and that's of the past for you. So he still has to grow, but while he's growing, he still has to learn from the past because if you don't know 1 2 3 and two 2s and rey rey rey he's going to flop. Learn from the past! So it doesn't just stop at 1 2 3. It goes way back to learn, hold it, music the best thing can unite them. Music unites them. Everything has to use sounds and words. That camera ain't got no flesh. That man and woman have sex, and a baby is born and that type of flesh, strength flesh, our flesh, the more flesh we have where you can record me and such and tape my voice. You don't have a tongue? Speakers speaking words, same words I speak. Some words are current.

So if I say a word is current to me the man who speaks the word what then? What am I then? Then how do you use the word? No, man. The speaker says, 'What did I say?' Cut up the speaker, does it have a tongue? It has none, so how the speaker - What am I going to do? Program myself, read book, read. Then anything I say it has to say. So ooh all right, walk away now. See what's happening now?

Set it nice and give it to the people, people love it and feed the people, and I say you can declare the most high work with it and call the people with it too. What? I wouldn't let go, hold onto it dada, bring it, come music. Sometimes the parents talk to the kid the kid don't listen, but if you put the message in a song and play the song your kid listens. Your kid don't follow what you say, but he'll go hear what a Rastaman wants to sing and sing it and come back in here, and you say, 'Okay, okay all right.' Sometimes you have to see the road a kid walks and put it in front of him too. Sometime another family might give it to your kid to how it stay, or sometimes some kid can get it from a next family and come back. So we want to praise the one Jah, so when the baby go out anywhere, he'll go buck up on the one God and him bring back the one clean knowledge same way. It's just how I see it.

Many youths I know have no place to go. A lot of people good and bad and let me tell you something, some people will tell me things they wouldn't say that to the President. Some people have told me things and have quarrelled with even me. 'Who are you trying to love them?' Say, 'Watch there.' Human beings, they are like water.

Man has become molecules, unstable, so you have to know how to deal with them to get them nice and make them happy and make them flow. So if you can't deal with people like that don't deal with people. People are like water. Deal with them nice and let them keep cool because it's a cycle. When they a pass you take something and watch it float. When they pass you give them what they should get to make them read and go on their way. That's how I deal with people. That's how I deal with David. I deal with David and such. Animals same way, it's a cycle. Something passes our Earth; it's time God gives them, a glory to see the Earth natural and current. Look at how much things have come and enjoyed the Earth. Right now robots can be on the Earth. Robots can walk right out there right now. We are like the satellite that has the navigation. So all you can do is program some little robots that work off the satellite, and it just starts walking upon the Earth, enjoying the Earth - rrrr rrrrrr. Robot rules the Earth, so why can't I float and enjoy the Earth? So the little human being, what's wrong with you my brother? Here's some money, go away.

That's how it is because robot a comes and enjoys what I should enjoy.

You have navigation, as well, brother, that you punch a number like this and that carries you where you go. All you have to do is stare. You have cars that don't need your navigation. It doesn't need you as a human being. The main guys that rule the world can program it and sit on it, and it just happens. Cars are driving the President around, wait on the President. All you have to do is be on time as well, that's what it has come to. Everything is just relaxation to make it easier for the human structure. When it comes back to everything go and make it easy for the human structure, so we have to live good because the wicked man is going to fail. The beast is going to fail and all the people that love to support the beast who don't fear God.

How will you prosper? I have to know you are a living human being and if you get cut you bleed, so I have to know that. No man, if I get a cut, I'm not like that. You can't cut the man because you must feel it by knowing it by your flesh alone before you inflict it on a next man. Even when he's a million times wrong, for me as the King you can't tell me anything. Even when the King says, 'And if he shall rise put him to death.' Yes, he should be put to death but hear me now, the only person who can tell me to put him to death is his mother and father. They brought him into the world. Do you think I carried him or her? In my country, if your mother and your father are not there no man can put you to death. When I come back as the King, and I take his life his mother and father have to say yes.

Hear how your judgment come, if your mother comes and cries against you and your father cries against you, we are going to say your mother hates you man. So even if we deal with it as brothers a part of us will not dwell with you because you have no current of respect ... So that's how I know that God says honour your mother and your father. Do you know what your mother's current is? You! Do you know what your father's current is? You! You should have it. That is what everyone uses to calculate. All the babies calculate with it and have a message for you and just love it. It brought me and I can do nothing about it. Babylon now is a different man. Now where is a man who loves death? Babylon tries to make death something that is still living. He will make all robots and even take your blood and clone you. He rules us now as Egyptian, you as American, Canadian ... Babylon rules us now. Anything Babylon does or says we have to follow.

If we tell our people, God says once you acknowledge the Sabbath that's it. Babylon makes some laws and disturbs many families and breaks down in certain evil ways. So they don't even remember that they exist with good ways. They don't remember anything about that. So you can't trouble them. You have to leave them. Once they are living leave them. They are still living, but at a time they are going to get up and attack someone else. What happened to that? And God still gives him life, he just killed someone, killed the most high saint and he still walks, and the life that he is walking with was created by God. How about that?

The same life is going to come out of a certain anointed flesh from Jah, the same way that it runs and holds him and says - It is still God in man the same way, so what I don't do another man will do. So I know that I will continue to do good. Some men will do good; some men will do bad according to the pleasure of the flesh to lead us astray to the pleasure of the flesh.

Right now, one of the sweetest pleasure is the pleasure of the words man, righteous words. I don't have to walk much if I read. If I don't read I will have to walk a lot because it's right there but because I don't read I'll walk to that point. I'll move like a fool. All I have to do is follow my father and just read, and when they say you know, it looks like you built the house, listens to this architect, you know it seems you can deal with the Doctor thing. So since you're humble for one hour, it's one hour you can read the Bible in an hour and then be humble for ten hours. Give him the Bible ten times then. So that's how the Rastaman ended up knowing it because Rastaman is a man who sits humble and knows that it's an eye for an eye and a tooth for a tooth - Moses law.

When Moses looks and sees that and says - Moses has to study in his realms too and says, 'How am I going to get these people to stop killing each other?' And the most high just ticked in Moses and just said, 'Moses, don't you see how I looked nice and she looked nice? Don't you see I said that they must look nice and praise me when they look good?' So are you going to do that? Moses just derived with his own natural thing from the most high's inspiration and said an eye for an eye and a tooth for a tooth. That means that if you don't cut me, then I won't cut you because I don't want to lose my eye I won't trouble your eye. So it's just I, I, I and I. I see it an live.

Love is his people and loves people, man. See people and love people. Before you even hate people and scorn people, love people then you will find out how to deal with them and how to manage them.

If you don't love it, you won't know where to place it. Sizzla Kalonji, yuh hear. Suh me stay. One love, yeah man.

Lindo P:
It's a blessing.

Sizzla:
Is a blessing to come through, man.

Lindo P:
What's going on with Judgement Yard?

Sizzla:
Judgement Yard? Right now I built a studio for Judgement Yard, and I'm making music long time, and I found out that when my records sell I get a lot of money, and when I get a lot of money I know that when my friends are hungry, and his family is sick I could give him a little of my money and I'm all right, and I didn't kill nor thief. Increased the talent pon dem! Reread the Bible, and the man said singing and playing of instruments my springs are in thee. I went back into the studio, and I saw some men making a rhythm. I said these men are lost, and they are still playing music? They said, 'Sizzla, what's up?' I said, 'What's up father?' I said, 'Yeah, I'm building a studio that means you all can dwell with me because you see me, you love me and come around me. When I see what you want to stay happy and I built a studio for Judgement.'
So do you see how the talent comes back now? So he loves the studio, so when he stays now, and his mind begins to stray, he probably does something wrong, Babylon locks him down and start, but dada doesn't have a studio man. 'Yow, come in my friend, what's up mi dups!' Boom bang, go up to dada, string up and start because the sound carries mind thought waves over the place and anything he plays on the music represents his mind and thoughts. So the nation follows his mind and talks through the music. Any other way they won't follow his mind and know what he's doing because he stays one way and he's blank. If he doesn't speak, you don't know. If he doesn't walk or do anything you don't know, and he can't think of bad, and you don't know. So when he sings, you can know what he thinks of the world. When he plays, you can know when he's thinking of the world. So he'll end up being back with King David.

When he plays his instrument and starts to play the melody, you can feel it and know it and say okay, and you understand the man more through the music.

So my yard is a yard that is just the Judgement I call it. So if you come and behave stupid fyah fi yuh, says me. My yard run mad still but under a conscious level because if I come there, there's a man washing his car and the music dum dum dum dum dum and another man comes in with 100 and says, 'Dada, I want two dubplates.' I say, 'Come in, man.' While he's up there washing his car my Engineer turns on the music in my studio and gets mad, and dada gets mad as well and, yow, money comes. Hold this money for a prescription; a baby was just born. Hmmm, hold that, and I say what do you mean by you're there on the money? Hmm, hold this. Don't you see we're not on the money? Hold this. By morning I stay there, and people call me again, and I start singing, and I get more money, and I sit back say hold on didn't I finish the money last night? Mi done the money last night, and I'll sit beside some youngsters now, and they're saying, 'Sizzla, can I get a five bills I'm starving. I'll be able to cook,' and I'm looking and I'm saying bomboclaat, if I can sing one song and get $5000 and just to say 'Praises', and I get $5000 much less a little baby that doesn't even know, you don't have to show the baby how to sing.

Let me tell you something, read the book and think of love and love them and remember. It's your son and your daughter, don't let them steal it. If they steal from you-you're going to lose. He learnt how to love it, so he learnt how to sing to keep it, and he learnt the music, and he started to be a little deejay. So when I have a studio, now it's easier for him because he doesn't have to go out on the road because if he goes to the studio, the Police will lock him up for a spliff in the car. He wants a spliff because God made the Earth and put the herbs on the Earth. So you have to go ask God why he put the herbs on the Earth.

When you quarrel with the Doctor because she found a certain cure for gonorrhoea, why are you quarrelling with me because I found certain plants that rise me to the realms? So the music is good, so I have to put things in place. If you're not putting things in place, you're a fuckery amongst the youths. That's how I see it. At that time I cuss pure bomboclaaat and get mad now because you see me as a fool. We see it. We've been through it. We get the chastisement. 'Aye boy, you're a liar. Why are you on the road? Are you a bad man?' And you see him beat me up.

Do you know why he is beating me up? It is because of my mother and father's principle that says I'm not to kill. He doesn't believe me that I'm not going to kill. He's holding to a principle too, and he beats me up with it. "Watch it, boy; you'll go to jail. You're a thief; you're a criminal, you're killing people.' We're not to kill. He's beating me up because of my mother and father's principles, and I'm still a killer and say Jah know, look at this? What is this? Look at that, and I'm smoking just a little spliff to sing a little thing. Sing what? The system set a way. So you see the only thing that Babylon listens to, and you know you're quick, it's through the music, so you have to put the youths there and let them know it is at BET, there they are MTV, VH1 there they are. Every little youth wants to start to sing now, and Babylon starts to make the phones with cameras and so the girls got away on me when I'm on the stage. Because at one point when the camera wasn't on the phone, and I was deejaying, nobody would come … Right now, I can't even move. People hang on even on my shirt to catch a picture. 'Hold on, King. Don't move.' Video, 'Say something to me, King.'

That what it has come to so I'm showing you what they want. The people want love. The people want to know I can leave my family with you and nothing.

goes wrong with my family. My daughter won't get raped; you won't kill and enslave my son. Soon come back.

If it's not like that it can't work, war. So we have to just set the music, that's why we're here. Represent with us. Represent each other. That's all we get out of it. They should give me some of the millions of dollars, and I'll show you what's going on. I'd build some big things in Africa too. That's what I'm talking about. Build even my own car, own guitar; I'll have my own piano because I have people who can play it. Make them too. Buy a machine that makes them and makes them too.

Lindo P:
Respect.

Sizzla:
It's all good, you know. Got a lot of things to cover but it's just the joy, Papaman. You wrote the Bible, and we are going to read it and know what's happening. So it's what I say that you will know.

Photos by Patrick Nichols

Album Discography

1995

- **Burning Up** (RAS Records)

1997

- **Black Woman & Child** (Digital B/Brickwall Records)
- **Praise Ye Jah** (XTerminator)

1998

- Sizzla & Anthony B - **2 Strong Series 1** (Star Trail)
- **Good Ways** (Digital B/Brickwall Records)

- **Kalonji** (XTerminator)
- **Freedom Cry** (VP Records)
- **Hotter Than Fire** (Genesis Records)

1999

- **Be I Strong** (VP Records)
- Sizzla, Anthony B, Luciano - **3 Wise Men: Love, Peace and Consciousness** (J&D Records)
- **Royal Son Of Ethiopia** (Greensleeves Records)

2000

- **Bobo Ashanti** (Greensleeves Records)
- **Liberate Yourself (One)** (Kariang Records)
- **Liberate Yourself (Two)** (Kariang Records)

2001

- **Taking Over** (VP Records)
- **Black History** (Jahmin' Records)
- **Rastafari Teach I Everything** (Greensleeves Records)
- Sizzla, Luciano, Anthony B - **We Three Kings** (Artists Only! Records)

2002

- **Hosanna** (Reggae Central)
- **Blaze Up The Chalwa** (Jet Star Records/Charm/King Of Kings)
- **Da Real Thing** (VP Records)
- **Ghetto Revolution** (Greensleeves Records)
- **Blaze Fire Blaze** (Whodat Records)
- **Up In Fire** (2B1 Records)

2003

- **Rise To The Occasion** (Greensleeves Records)

- **African Children** (Fire Ball Records)
- **Light Of My World** (Charm)
- **Red Alert** (Jet Star Records)
- **Ever So Nice**
- Sizzla, Luciano, Mikey General, Anthony B - **4 Rebels Vol. 2** (RAS Records)

2004

- **Life** (Greensleeves Records)
- Sizzla & Luciano - **Jah Warrior** (Penitentiary Records)
- **Speak Of Jah** (Bogalusa)
- **Stay Focus** (VP Records/XTerminator)
- **Brighter Day** (Kingston Records)
- **Jah Knows Best** (Sanctuary Records)
- **Kings Of Dancehall** (Charm)
- **Stay Focus** (VP Records/XTerminator)

2005

- **Burning Fire** (Penitentiary Records)
- **Soul Deep** (Greensleeves Records)

2006

- **Jah Protect** (Penitentiary Records)
- **The Overstanding** (Damon Dash Music Group)
- **Ain't Gonna See Us Fall** (VP Records)
- **Waterhouse Redemption** (Greensleeves Records)
- **Esta Loca "Bless The Mixtapes"** (Dance Factory)

2007

- **Children Of Jah** (Rude Boy Records)

- **I-Space** (Greensleeves Records)

2008

- **Rastafafari** (Penitentiary Records)
- **Stand Tall** (Yes Records)
- **Addicted** (Drop Di Bass Records)

2009

- **Ghetto Youth-Ology** (Greensleeves Records)

2010

- **Crucial Times** (Greensleeves Records)

2011

- **The Scriptures** (John John Records)
- **In Gambia** (Kalonji Records)

2012

- **The Chant** (Afrojam Music)

2013

- **The Messiah** (VP Records)

2014

- Sizzla & Mista Savona - **Born A King** (Multi Music)

2016

- **876** (Judgement Yard/868 Music)
- **Good Ways**
- **Trod The Valley** (Judgement Yard)

Review Plea

Thank you for reading my book.

I appreciate all of your comments, and I love hearing what you have to say. I need your comments to make the next book in this series better.

Please leave a helpful review wherever you got this copy letting me know what you thought of this book.

Thanks so much!

Who Is Harris Rosen?

Father. Son. Brother.

Harris Rosen is the author of N.W.A: The Aftermath, The Real Eminem: Broke City Trash Rapper, and other Behind The Music Tales books. For twenty years, he self-published the national lifestyle magazine Peace! He lives in Toronto, Canada, with his son, Louis.

Rosen has interviewed hundreds of composers, artists, actors, and athletes. Including the Notorious B.I.G., Dr Dre, Daft Punk, Eminem, Derek Jeter, Georges St. Pierre, Nirvana, Metallica, Chris Rock, Buju Banton, Beastie Boys, Kiss, Destiny's Child and Aaliyah to list a few.

He has gone to six continents and was in the midst of a whirlwind of multiple musical, cultural revolutions that occurred throughout the 90's and 2000s while compiling a genuine and honest archive of audio, images and video.

Twitter.com/mrheller1
Facebook.com/behindthemusictales
Instagram.com/harrisrosenbtmt
behindthemusictales.com

Behind The Music Tales Books

N.W.A: The Aftermath

The Real Eminem: Broke City Trash Rapper

The Real Destiny's Child: The Writing's On The Wall

New York State of Mind 1.0

Magnolia: Home of tha Soldiers (Behind the Scenes with the Cash Money Millionaires)   The Real 213

The Real MC Eiht: Geah!

The Real Diddy

The Real Daft Punk

BEHINDTHEMUSICTALES.COM

BEHINDTHEMUSICTALES.COM

www.ingramcontent.com/pod-product-compliance
Lightning Source LLC
Chambersburg PA
CBHW061929290426
44113CB00024B/2858